BUILDING A
POWERFUL TEAM
A SMALL BUSINESS GUIDE TO CREATING
SUPERSTAR EMPLOYEES

by

EMERY V. BROWN

TABLE OF CONTENTS

DON'T BE A SUPERHERO

If you're a small business owner or entrepreneur, you know what it means to build a business from the ground up. It takes smart thinking, ingenuity, and a ton of hard work to create a successful business.

Many small business owners are very protective of their vision because they know exactly where they want to take their business. Sooner or later, though, most entrepreneurs recognize that they need help to grow.

They can work 80 hours a week, but in order to meet the demands of their business, it's going to take a team.

If you're ready to start growing your work team, this book will give you the skills to find an incredible team and the knowledge to create a productive work environment.

Avoid the Hero Complex and Build a Team

You may be the type of person who does everything for themselves. You trust yourself the most, you're the one who understands your vision the most, and you're the best person to see that vision come to fruition.

That's a good plan if you have a very small business that depends solely on your own efforts. There are some small businesses that *can* be run by one person.

However, if you want to significantly expand your business, you're probably going to need help.

For most businesses, great success arises from having an incredible team of workers - a group of people who:

- Understand and share your values
- Have a strong work ethic
- Have the skills to push things forward

Have you ever heard of "superhero syndrome?"

Superhero syndrome means that you feel that you're the only one who can do things well — and you *should* be the one doing everything.

In his book *Virtual Freedom,* Chris Ducker writes,

> *...your business is your baby, and who better to take care of that baby than the person who gave birth to it -- you! However, this will eventually catch up with you, and the strength that you*

possess as an entrepreneur will start to backfire...[It] will leave you stressed and overworked, and ultimately, you will be no good to anyone or anything -- including your business.

Chris Ducker isn't the only one to recognize the need for a strong team. Outsourcing work is critical to the success of countless businesses -- small and large.

Hillary Kerr and Katherine Power are the creators of the extremely popular blog *Who What Wear.* What started as a small newsletter eventually expanded into a highly lucrative and successful blogging business.

But they certainly didn't do it alone.

In an interview with *Fashionista*, Hillary Kerr answered the question, "How do you manage to juggle all of [your] different projects at the same time?

She said:

And as we continue to grow, it's always hard to let go of certain aspects of your job that you like and projects that you want to be super involved in but don't have the time to be. Having the right team in place for us in our company has also been huge. But also thinking, 'Is this something that only I can do? Or is this something that I can delegate to another really wonderful team member?' It's been a balancing act and I think it will continue to be.

Bill Gates, the founder of Microsoft, used to have a big challenge with delegating work to his team. When he first started his company, he struggled to trust his employees and had a strong urge to micromanage.

When his company first launched, he wrote most of the code and he re-wrote or reviewed everyone else's as well.

His need to manage everything began to affect his company's productivity.

Over time, he realized that this was not the best thing for him or the company. He began trusting others to manage new hires, write code, market his products, and many other things. He even began to realize that some of the people who worked for him were *better* than he was.

If you're an entrepreneur, establishing a good team is key to your overall success.

In this book, you'll learn how to establish the kind of team that you need for a successful, productive, and profitable business.

HOW TO FIND GOOD PEOPLE

You know you need help, but how do you decide what's missing from your business?

Before you can hire the perfect team, you'll need to determine exactly what you need help with.

Do you need employees who can take over some of your responsibilities, or do you need to hire people with expertise that you don't currently have?

At some point, you'll probably need some of both.

Determine What Your Business Is Missing

Here are some quick and simple ways to know when it's time to expand:

- You're not able to do big tasks because you're spending all your time on rote work or focusing on small details.

- Your customers are not getting the attention they need.

- You have steady, consistent work - not just a week or two of intense work.

- You or your current staff are consistently overworked and frustrated.

- Hiring new people will increase revenue.

- You're turning down work because you can't keep up.

- You need someone to do a specialized task.

- You're making enough money to hire employees.

Having a few busy weeks doesn't necessarily mean that it's time to hire additional employees. Taking on a full-time employee would be a mistake if you can't provide them with ongoing work. You don't want to pay a salary to someone who is often sitting around with nothing to do.

If you need occasional help finishing something, you may want to look into freelance workers or contractors. You can also hire consultants to help with specialized skills.

But if you have enough money in the budget and a new employee will help increase revenue, it's probably a good time to bring on a new hire.

You may only need part-time help at first, but as your business continues to grow, those positions will turn into full-time work.

How to Find Applicants That Can Benefit Your Company

Many experienced entrepreneurs have been burned by bad employees. This can cause some businesspeople to want to avoid hiring anyone. Instead of starting the cycle of hiring again, they buckle down - determined to do the work themselves.

An incompetent or unethical employee is difficult to forget, but it shouldn't cause you to be filled with fear. There are good workers out there who are ready to support your business -- you just have to find them.

Here are five important things to consider when bringing on a new employee.

Define Your Business Culture

Have you ever heard the term "workplace culture"? It may sound strange or even kitschy, but the idea behind it is extremely important.

The culture of your company is a combination of:

- Values
- Traditions
- Behaviors
- Attitudes
- Beliefs

The culture can be positive or negative, and **you have the power to guide it.** The people you hire will also have a lot to do with your business' culture.

In order to maintain the type of culture that you want, it's important to hire people that will enhance it instead of diminishing it.

Look for people who share your values and understand the vision and branding that you have for your company.

For example, imagine that you started a business selling outdoor camping gear. You decided to focus heavily on going green and your company's eco-impact.

When you hire employees for your business, you would want to hire people who are knowledgeable about outdoor gear and also care about the environment. That's the culture that you would be cultivating.

A person with zero experience in camping or a person who doesn't care about green living wouldn't fit into your culture.

Hire People of Strong Integrity and Character

Your employees should be knowledgeable about your products, but they should also be ethical people who can work well with others. More than anything, you want to avoid hiring toxic people who will cause division or harm fellow employees.

Billionaire and CEO of Berkshire Hathaway, Warren Buffett, once said:

> We look for three things when we hire people. We look for intelligence, we look for initiative or energy, and we look for integrity. And if they don't have the latter, the first two will kill you, because if you're going to get someone without integrity, you want them lazy and dumb.

Buffett was making the point that **integrity is more important than simply having a smart or energized employee.**

Hiring trustworthy employees means you can unburden some of your responsibilities without fear.

It also means that you're providing other employees with a safe work environment. Your workplace should be sensitive to your employees' unique needs and have a low risk for things like sexual harassment or discrimination.

Consider these questions to help determine if your new hire has the kind of integrity you need for your business:

- Do they have a positive attitude at work, or are they always complaining and bringing down the morale?

- Are they able to communicate openly?

- Do they follow through with commitments?

- If they tell you they will do something, do they try their best to do it?

- Are they able to hold themselves accountable? In other words, do they continue to do work well even when you're not present?

- Are they willing to take responsibility for their actions?

- Do they always blame others when something goes wrong?

- Do they spend their time building up others or do they tear others down?

- Are they more concerned with their ego or the good of the company and the team?

No employee is going to be perfect, but a team member that works with integrity will produce ongoing rewards.

Almost everyone recognizes a person of character and this attribute will go well beyond your workforce. Your customer base will also respect a company that hires trustworthy people.

Create a Diverse Team of Workers

Today's business world is recognizing the need for diversity in the workplace. The business landscape has been changing over the past sixty years and many companies are learning that diversity is a strength rather than a weakness.

A diverse work team has many benefits, including:

- Increased productivity

- More creativity and out-of-the-box thinking
- Greater innovation
- Faster problem solving
- Reduced employee turnover
- Marketing that is more inclusive and sensitive to various demographics
- Enhanced company reputation

Diversifying your business is not necessarily an easy task, however. People who are similar tend to spend time with others like themselves. That makes it harder to find new or different types of people.

If you want to bring in people from many demographics, there are a few things you can do:

1. **Make diversity a part of your business culture.** Before you begin hiring new employees, resolve to make your business culture vibrant. **You want people who have common goals but avoid confusing that with hiring people**

who are all the same.

2. **Determine your criteria before the interview.** To prevent a subconscious bias when interviewing and hiring, choose your criteria *before* you begin interviewing. That will help you treat all applicants in an unbiased way.

3. **Have a diverse group of people interviewing.** When you interview, have others on the panel besides yourself. Invite people from different demographics to help you choose employees.

4. **Post job opportunities in diverse localities.** In addition to where you would normally post a job opening, pick non-traditional places to post your job openings too, even if they don't seem like an obvious choice for your business.

5. **Attend job fairs in different communities.** Go to job fairs in communities and at colleges that have a more diverse population. You can also go to non-profit organizations that advocate for those who are ordinarily underrepresented.

Use a Variety of Avenues to Find Good People

You may know exactly what kind of people you want, but how do you actually find them?

The best way to recruit new people is to use a variety of avenues, such as:

1. **Personal network.** Chances are you've built up relationships with customers, clients, and business partners. Use those relationships to ask for referrals and recommendations. They may know the perfect person for your business.

2. **Social networks.** LinkedIn is a well-known resource for finding good help, but you can also use a social media platform like Facebook.

3. **Online job boards.** Popular job boards you can try are Flexjobs, Indeed, and CareerBuilder.

   - If you work in a niche industry, it's probably better to find a more specific job board. For example, if you work in tech, you may want to try Dice.com. If you're looking for a writer, you can try ProBlogger's job board. Efinancial Careers is good if you're looking for people that work in finance.

4. **Carry a business card with you.** Whether you're traveling the world for business or just stopping in at your local coffee shop, you never know when

there might be an opportunity to reach out to a potential hire.

Use Your Branding in Your Recruiting Ads

When posting an ad for your job opening, such as online, in newspapers, or on a physical job board, **remember that branding is important.** You may not be selling a product, but you are selling your company.

If you want to attract amazing applicants, give them a reason to want to apply. Try to think of creative ads that will get them interested in your business, as well as give them a clear idea of your company's ideals. That will also help lower the number of applicants that are a poor fit.

Thank You

THE IMPORTANCE OF MAKING YOUR EMPLOYEES FEEL VALUED

Finding the right employee is only part of the process of developing a powerful team of workers.

You may have excellent employees, but if they're not managed well, your business will struggle.

Treating Employees Well Benefits You and Your Company

The importance of treating your employees well can't be underestimated. You may not be able to make your employees millionaires, but the way you treat them makes a lasting difference.

In fact, how you treat your employees often affects the morale of the company more than the individual income levels. Certainly, compensating your employees well is important, but how you treat them may even be more important than high pay.

In 2015, *Harvard Business Review* published an article called "Proof that Positive Work Cultures are More Productive." They concluded that cut-throat, high-pressure business cultures are less effective than inclusive businesses that prioritize their employee's needs.

Why?

In the short term, your business may thrive under high-pressure management. Your employees may work twice as hard to meet your rising expectations.

In the long term, however, there are significant consequences to the high pressure, specifically:

- High healthcare costs and increased health issues among employees
- Disengagement among employees
- Lost loyalty – high turnover rate

Let's look at these consequences in greater detail.

Health Issues with High-Stress Jobs

The number one issue that arises from high- stress businesses is the toll it takes on your employee's health.

A study conducted by BMC Public Health concluded that individuals who work at high to medium strain jobs visit their general practitioners 26% more than those who work at low-pressure jobs. They also go to a specialist 27% more often.

Studies such as this show us that, in order to present a safe and healthy working environment for employees, **it's important to take note of the mental, physical, and emotional strain of the job.**

Disengagement

Workers who are disengaged are less likely to perform well, and far more likely to have an accident or make a mistake.

Here are some surprising statistics about disengaged workers:

- 89% of employers think employees leave because of money when, in fact, only 12% leave primarily for better pay.

- Companies with engaged employees make 2.5x more revenue.

- Employees who are highly engaged are 87% less likely to leave their company.

- It's estimated that disengaged employees cost organizations between $450 and $550 billion annually.

- Fewer than three out of ten employers have an engagement strategy.

Lost Loyalty

High-stress jobs also lead to high turnover rates. Employees don't feel loyal to jobs that leave them feeling unhealthy and unappreciated.

According to the American Institute of Stress, the number one cause of stress in people's lives is their workloads. They also said that 19% of people polled had quit a previous job due to stress.

The cost of replacing an employee is high and should be avoided when possible.

So, how can you be sure that you're treating your employees well?

How to Make Employees Feel Valued

To help your employees feel like they're a valuable member of the team, there are a lot of things that you can do.

Here are some **highly effective ways to let your employees know that you care about them** and you're glad that they're part of the team:

1. **Compensate them well.** You don't have to pay your employees so well that you forfeit a healthy budget. However, paying your employees a fair wage will go a long way. You may only have jobs that would normally pay minimum wage, but a small bump up from that would mean a lot to your employees.

2. **Offer flexibility.** There are a growing number of employees who really desire flexibility in their work schedule. A study from the *Harvard Business Review* said that 96% of US professionals want flexibility in their schedule, but only 47% feel that they have it in their current position.

  - While a 9-5 job was once the norm, this is changing with younger generations. Employees want the option to have a flexible schedule that fits their lifestyle. They want the freedom to work a different shift or work changing shifts based on their needs.

  - **Many applicants are looking for jobs that allow them to work remotely, or to have the ability to work from home some of the time.**

3. **Listen to your employees and show them that you care.** Taking the time to listen to the people who work for you will make a difference in how they feel about their time at work.

   - Do your best to give them your undivided attention. Set the phone down, walk away from the computer, and let them know you're paying attention by looking at them and being present. If you're completely unavailable at the time, schedule a time that you can speak with them.

4. **Show your employees appreciation.** Almost everyone needs to feel that the work they do is seen and appreciated. Some personality types need more affirmation than others, but **most people need to know that the work they do is important and valued.**

- A survey conducted by Glassdoor found that over half of the people surveyed said they would stay at their company longer if they felt appreciated by their boss.

5. **Have reasonable expectations.** It's easy to feel like your employees have easy jobs. It's especially true if it's something that you've been doing well for a long time. While you certainly don't want to employ people who are completely incompetent, remember that people learn and acquire skills at different rates.

   - Something that you're completely comfortable doing may take a new employee some time to master.

   - Be patient with them while they're learning and refrain from becoming easily annoyed.

6. **Teach your employees well the first time.** It's far better to teach them well at the beginning than to have to keep retraining them on the same tasks.

  - Plus, they'll feel like you've taken the time to work with them rather than rushing through important information that they need to know for their jobs.

7. **Don't be afraid to loosen up a little.** Work is a place of work. But there's also power in play.

  - Google, one of the most successful tech companies in the world, knows the value of happy employees. They allow employees to bring their pets to work. They also offer gyms and swimming pools, video games, foosball tables, and loads of other perks.

- You may not be able to give your employees as many perks as Google, but you can take a page out of their handbook. **Giving your employees time to have fun can have substantial benefits.**

CREATE A GREAT
WORKPLACE CULTURE

In addition to finding employees that fit your culture, you also want to cultivate a culture that people work well in. Treating your employees well is a great first start, but there's more to managing a great team than just being kind.

Here are a few practical ways that you can help grow a workplace culture that's functional, sustainable, and productive.

Create Clear Roles and Expectations

When you bring on a new hire, **it's imperative that they understand their roles and responsibilities.** It's your job to define them clearly so everyone is on the same page.

When a job description is vague or open to interpretation, it can often become confusing and frustrating. Your employees may try to do things you don't want them to, or they may not be doing tasks you do expect them to do. This also opens the door for unnecessary conflicts with you and their fellow employees.

The problem is compounded when you don't have an effective management system in place. Without adequate leadership, teamwork suffers because no one knows who is in charge.

Be very clear with your employees about the hierarchy of management.

If you're the only person in a leadership role, ensure that the rest of the employees understand that they are on a level playing field.

Before you post a job position, determine exactly what you need help with. Include this in the job description. **The skills you require should make reasonable sense and match the pay scale.**

For example, if you're hiring someone primarily to answer the phones, you probably can't reasonably expect them to also be a tech whiz and run your cybersecurity.

It isn't fair to current or future employees to give them responsibilities that are far outside of their experience, and you can't expect them to do high-level work for low-level pay.

If you feel that your employees are outgrowing their current position, consider promoting them.

Try to avoid tacking on a never-ending list of responsibilities to a strong employee. If you're giving them more and more responsibilities, then the pay and title should match.

Give Employees a Sense of Purpose

Andrew Sillitoe is a business psychologist who believes that **in order for a company to be a high-performance business, employees must feel like they have a purpose.**

More and more, people want to do more than a punch in and punch out. They want to feel like the work they do is meaningful and purpose driven.

Sillitoe has outlined five major areas of change that can be used in the workplace:

1. **Shaping the story.** Let them help create the story of your business. Your employees want to feel like they're part of the mission of your business, so allow them to have a say in the direction.

2. **Ask, don't tell.** Instead of telling your employees everything they should be doing, ask them questions. For example: What do they think can be done to improve their own performance? What would make it easier for them to do their jobs?

3. **Create leaders.** You want people to follow your directions, but you also want them to be able to lead. **Leaders are able to influence change and foster a high-performance culture.**

4. **Embrace failure.** It's important for your business to work smoothly, but your employees shouldn't be afraid of failing. There will be times that they make mistakes and they shouldn't live in fear when they do.

   - If they're innovative, they're also likely to try some things that don't work. However, your forward-thinking employees are also the ones that are going to help your business grow. So, give them the opportunity to try new ideas.

5. **Hold each other accountable.** Holding your employees accountable is a necessary part of being their boss. However, without the other steps, your employees will feel controlled instead of being part of a team.

   - **You want them to feel like you're working together towards a**

united goal. That's why they need a purpose *before* you can hold them accountable.

Help Your Employees Work Together

To create a harmonious work culture, you also want your employees to work together.

Here are some practical ways that you can keep teamwork strong:

1. **Strengthen your leadership.** A team without strong leadership struggles to thrive. Leaders should set an example for the rest of the employees. **Their job is to show best practices to the rest of**

the employees. They're also present to settle disputes and create open communication among workers.

- If your leadership team struggles to get along or work together, it will be much harder for the rest of your workers to get along with each other as well.

2. **Team building retreats and activities.** Team building activities may make your employees feel like rolling their eyes, but these exercises can be extremely beneficial. They help break down barriers between employees, give them a common goal, and give them time to work together in unique ways.

- Some team building activities are ineffective and actually embarrass workers. Before you start making adults put together towers made of spaghetti and marshmallows, ask what your goals are.

- **Think about your goals ahead of time and ensure that your activities reinforce your vision.**

- You may want to involve team building professionals to help develop a program that will be effective for your company.

3. **Keep everyone on the same page.** From entry-level positions all the way up to upper management, your work team should have the same mission. Each member should be given a clear understanding of how they can be a part of that mission.

   - When everyone is working towards the same ultimate goal, it's much easier for your workforce to work together as a team.

4. **Include ideas from all levels of employees.** You do want to have a clear understanding of leadership roles in your business, but that doesn't mean low-level employees can't contribute.

- **Let *all your employees* know that they have a say in the business and that leadership is willing to listen to their ideas.**

    You may be surprised by how much your employees are willing and able to offer.

5. **Encourage employees to communicate with each other.** You can foster good employee relationships by offering social events where they can get to know each other on a personal level. Give them time to share lunch breaks and throw work socials.

- Another thing you can do is give them time to work together on projects. This is a simple way to encourage people to get to know each other at work and develop lasting relationships.

START BUILDING YOUR TEAM TODAY

This book references many successful businesses. While your business may not currently be able to offer perks like Google, or be as famous as Microsoft, the fundamentals are the same.

You want to hire a team of people who are smart and work hard, but **it's also essential that they fit into your workplace culture.** Some of this you will have to determine from your gut. That's the part that can't be analyzed or formulated from the outside.

When you meet or interview someone, do you feel deep down that they will be an asset to your team? Your gut won't always be right, but you're the most qualified person to assess what your business needs.

Once you've accumulated a strong team, remember to treat them well. Making your employees feel valued and part of an important mission doesn't have to be complicated.

Simply treating them with kindness, listening to their concerns, and making them feel like they're part of a team will put you beyond many other businesses.

People want to feel like their work is meaningful and appreciated. It doesn't take loads of money or time to make your team feel like you care -- and the benefits of this will be far-reaching and long-lasting.

Finally, give them an amazing culture to work in. Give them the opportunity to pitch ideas, work their way up to leadership roles, and have the freedom to make mistakes in the name of progress. Encourage your employees to spend time with each other and help them learn to collaborate on projects.

If you hire people with integrity and give them a productive, supportive working environment, there's no end to the new levels your business can reach.